# Mom & Dad: A Memory Revisited

## Jeanette Davis Norris

BK

ROYSTON
Publishing

BK Royston Publishing
P. O. Box 4321
Jeffersonville, IN  47131
http://www.bkroystonpublishing.com
bkroystonpublishing@gmail.com

© Copyright – 2023

Cover Photo:  Jeanette Davis Norris

ISBN-13:  978-1-959543-65-7

Printed in the United States of America

# Dedication

THIS BOOK IS DEDICATED

MY MOM AND DAD

ROSELLA DAVIS

&

DENNIS L. DAVIS

# Table of Contents

# Introduction

It was September 6, 2021, the day before my birthday. Sixty-eight years before that, on the same day, Monday September 6, 1954, my parents went to the beach, an event that we always celebrated on Labor Day. Labor Day was always celebrated on the first Monday of the month of September. We are here again on the exact date but a different year. My last trip to Miami to see Mom and take care of her. (I did not know at the time, but God did). My brother called me at work to say that he did not like how Mom was looking, so I suggested to him to call the ambulance and have them take her to the hospital. We had just signed papers for her to be put under hospice care a few days before. They were there, making her comfortable. My brother waited anxiously for my opinion, and he hung up from me and called them.

They admitted Mom, and I was on the first flight the next morning. Only one visitor was allowed at a time, for one hour, so the nurses allowed me to stay if I wanted to. I would come back the next day and the next day, which brings me to the Sunday before Labor Day. I visited Mom and was talking to her about the next day being Labor Day. I reminded her how she would always tell me, year after year for as long as I could remember, how she and

Dad would go to the beach on Labor Day, and here we are, sixty-seven years ago on Sunday, the day before Labor Day, September 6. When they arrived home, Mom laid across the bed, and when she woke up, her water broke. They went to the hospital, and I was born around 5:40 the next morning. I told Mom I was going to the beach today and spend the day there, just like she and Dad did sixty-seven years ago.

# Chapter One

Toot toot!! The sound of the horn on the bus that holds fifteen to eighteen small children, was Jackson Toddle Inn. The kindergarten that my sister and I attended at the age of five. I can hear that horn every morning, in the middle of the street. All the kids who attended that school would run from their homes into the street to get on the bus. The bus would wait for a few minutes, until all the kids got on. It drove off to Jackson Toddle Inn where we learned how to read, write and do arithmetic. We had fun at that school. There were celebrations throughout the year. It was run by Mr. and Mrs.

Jackson, who were working together along with other teachers. I think it was only a preschool and kindergarten school. Most of the kids on Sixty-Eighth Street attended that school It was a private preschool and kindergarten where parents had to pay a tuition. Our family was middle class. My father, Dennis Davis, worked, but my mom, Rosella Davis, didn't. She raised us, kept the house clean, combed and plaited our hair, and bought our clothes. We dressed alike even though we weren't twins. We were two years apart. We attended the church down the street, where my father was an usher for many years and my mom sang in the choir. The name of the church was Mt. Moriah Baptist Church. I got baptized at that church at the age of nine. My god sister, Gwendolyn—we called her Gwen for short—got baptized around that same time, along with my sister who followed suit. Gwen attended New Mt Moriah Baptist Church, where her grandfather was the pastor for many years. She lived with her mom and dad and eight siblings. We had to sit on the morning bench, which was the first set of seats up front. Our dad would put us there at the beginning of service and he would come back and get us at the end of service. We were not allowed to sit anywhere else until we were baptized. We did not move, until our dad came and got us. After we got baptized, then we sang in the choir or ushered on the usher board. This all began when my father, who was born in Dawson, Georgia, came to Miami, Florida to work with his uncle, at the age of eighteen. He only finished third grade. He had to work to help the family. Dad had a dog named Butch. He left a girlfriend in Dawson, Georgia, and told her he was going to Miami to work and would come back and marry her. Well, that plan didn't work. My parents met one day when my mom was walking down the street on her way to the store, and my dad drove slowly by then asked her if she wanted a ride. They started dating and my dad had to ask my grandfather to marry her. My father would take the whole family to the beach on holidays, the Fourth of July and in September, Labor Day. I never forgot that my mother told me when I was born, she was sitting on the edge of the bed, feeding me, when she felt the end of the bed sink, as if someone was sitting at the edge. Not long after that, we got word that my grandmother, my dad's mother had passed.

# Chapter Two

My mom always thought that was her spirit visiting me. I was born the day after Labor Day. As I said, my dad would always take the family to the beach. Mom came home from the beach and rested across the bed because she was tired. She woke up and discovered her water had broken. During that time, you would have to call the funeral home to transport you to the hospital. They had an ambulance service, Range Funeral Home. They took my mom to the hospital, and I was born. While in the hospital, my parents did not have a name for a girl because they were expecting a boy. The nurse at the hospital suggested to my mom to name me after her, Jeanette. My middle name came from my father's sister, Louise.

My grandfather, Joseph Pierce, was from Haiti. He came over in a boat with his brother. They spoke another language, Creole. We would hear him speak it with his friends on the porch. He was much older than my grandmother. Joseph worked with my grandmother's father, Joseph Levarity. My grandfather was married before and had two children, Walter and Gladys. Walter lived in New York City, as well as Gladys, but we never met Gladys. She moved out of the home and went her own way. We have never seen her since. My grandfather asked my great-grandfather for my grandmother's hand in marriage. My grandmother, at that time, was thirteen years old. She had only one child, Rosella, who is my mother. Later, my grandfather built on to their home, and my dad, mom and two children, Jeanette Louise and Bonnie Denise, resided in the larger side of the house. We were not allowed to bother our grandparents and go on their side, but we would, anyway, when our dad wasn't home. When we heard the car pull in the driveway, we would run back to our side and pretend like we didn't go over on their side. My grandmother was the oldest of sixteen children, and her parents lived on the next street. They would make a pathway from our great-grandparents' house to theirs. My aunts and uncles would walk that path to visit their older sister, Isabell. Isabell and Joseph were great cooks. She would make coconut candy from scratch. He would cook Sunday dinners. You could always go to their house and there was something cooking or something to eat. Every Sunday, she would bake a cake or a pie.

My sister, Bonnie, and I would play together. The house we lived in and shared with our grandparents was fenced. We would play outside until almost dark. There was a cherry tree in the yard next door. We would take our hands and put it through the fence and pick the cherries off the tree. They would grow plentiful. They started out green, then turned yellow, then orange, then finally a sweet red. Sometimes we would pick them and eat them before they turned red. In the front and back yard, there were mango trees, with different kinds of mangoes in the front and the back. The long ones were called banana mangoes. The smaller, round ones were called turpentine ones. We loved to eat the mangoes. They would fall off the tree into the yard when they were ripe. Sometimes, my grandfather would take a long stick and pull them down. Outside the yard, there was a kiwi tree and coconut tree. We would break open the coconuts and drink the milky substance inside then open the coconut, pounding it on the sidewalk, and eat the inside. These fruits were plentiful to eat. Everybody either had a mango, avocado, coconut, kiwi, or a fruit tree. Neighbors would share their fruits and children ate them all day long. If we went visiting to friends' homes, we got some fruit from them depending on what they had. It was nothing to eat fruit all day and play outside until the streetlight came on.

# Chapter Three

My mom was an only child, born to the marriage of Joseph Pierce and Isabell Levarity. She was born in Miami, Florida. Mom went to school with her friends who lived in the area. They attended Dorsey High School.

One good friend was Vivian Hayes. They were very close, even after they were adults. Vivian Hayes married, and her name became Vivian Sippio. She had nine children. Eight boys and one girl. Mrs. Sippio and my mom would be on the phone talking every day.

There was another friend who lived on the same street, a couple of doors down. Her name was Mary Roker, and she lived with her one brother and four sisters. They lived with their mother and father. There was another friend; her name was Nellie Barr, and she lived nearby. As the school years went, they became good friends and attended the same schools until graduation. They continued their friendship in their adult years. They all got married and had children.

Mary Roker and my mom were on the drill team. They would always attend the games and perform, but when the team won, they would have a dance at the Liberty City Community Center. They had to be home before midnight.

There was one dance, Mary and my mom did not keep track of the time. They were dancing so much and having a good time when they realized it was midnight already. They were thinking about how much trouble they were going to get into because they were not home by twelve. My grandfather came to the center to get my mom. Mary's dad was waiting for her at home. She came up with the idea that she could change the time on the clock so her dad wouldn't know what time she came in. He was right there watching her trying to change the time. Her punishment was not to ever go to another dance.

My mom would pick up Mary on her way to school, and her dog Butch would sometimes tag along. They talked about how they got in trouble the night before. My mom was very shy and quiet. Mary's mom would always speak to Mom when she came to pick up Mary, but Mom was soft-spoken and polite, especially in front of other people.

They went to the football games and Mom would always have money and buy her friends some candy. They did what all high school friends did, attended different events at school and went to the prom. They got married and had children and continued to be friends as the years went on.

# Chapter Four

My mom joined New Birth Baptist Church. She would sing in the Wisdom Choir and joined the Silent Praise Ministry. They would take turns each Sunday to sign what the ministers would preach. Mom enjoyed being in the Silent Praise Ministry. She would pick up another friend of hers who attended the same church, Mrs. Elizabeth B. Finnie, whom they met in 1999. Mom always wanted a Cadillac. She even bought a 2003 Cadillac DeVille. Mom and Ms. Liz became good friends. They would go shopping together and Mom always left home early on Sundays to beat the crowd.

She liked getting the closer parking space at church. One Sunday, Mom got to church so early and could not understand why no one was there. Ms. Liz told Mom they are still at home, asleep.

There was another event at Parrot Jungle. When mom and Ms. Liz arrived, the employees were still setting up. It was too early. Mom believed in being on time.

One event was going on at the church, and Mom made the corsages for everyone. During an Easter celebration, she made Easter baskets for the children. They cancelled the event, but she was able to give the other children in the neighborhood the baskets. Ms. Liz said Mom was generous and would always remember her birthday. She remembered everybody's birthday and made them feel special.

Mom was generous to all her friends. Not only did she remember their birthdays, but their children's birthdays and holiday time, too. Mom met Ms. Annie Washington at Jackson High School. They became close friends. Sometimes when the weather was bad, mom would go stay the night with Ms. Washington. She was always afraid of lightning. She would make us get on the floor when bad weather occurred and be quiet until it was over.

Other women she befriended, were Mrs. Catherine Middleton, Ms. Sandra McElroy, and Ms. Tate. She would take care of her neighbors on her street and send cards and flowers as needed.

My father grew up in Dawson, Georgia, where he was raised by his grandmother. Dad got baptized in a lake not far from where he lived. Dad had a dog name Rover. They would go hunting for rabbits, squirrels and other animals in the woods. My dad would walk to school, but he quit when he entered third grade. He had to work in the field to help the family. I remember him telling me about his cousin, Trudie Bee, who could run faster than any of her siblings or cousins. My dad would get in trouble, and his grandmother would tell Trudie Bee to go get him. She ran faster than any of the other children, so she was always able to catch him and bring him back to Grandma. When Dad reached the age of seventeen, he decided to go to Daytona Beach, Florida and visit his uncle. This was the last time he left home. He stayed there about a year, but he and his cousin got into it, and he moved out and got a room and a steady job. He did several jobs in the community and eventually moved to Miami, Florida. He visited his friend,

Aunt Trudie Bee's husband. He thought they were still together. That's when he met my mom.

My grandfather on my dad's side was Emmitt Davis. My grandfather had seventeen children. Mattie Mae, Dennis (my dad), Louise, Mary, John Lee, Jim (Jimmy Lee), Mae (Jessie Mae), Ann (Annie Bell), Emmitt, Kate (Martha Kate), Earl, Lois (Jennifer), Eddie, Frank (Jerry), Pearl (Eva), Hattie Mae, and Charlie. I would always hear about him but thought he had passed on. We were visiting my aunts and uncles in Georgia when my Aunt Louise told us that my grandfather was not feeling well. I inquired and we went to see him. When we arrived, most of his children were there visiting too. My dad went with us, and I met my grandfather for the first time. He was blind at the time, and we took pictures and talked. He died a few months later, and I attended the funeral. I became really close to an uncle, Earl Davis, who met my dad for the first time that same day we visited. I met some of my other aunts and uncles, too. My grandfather had a total of seventeen children.

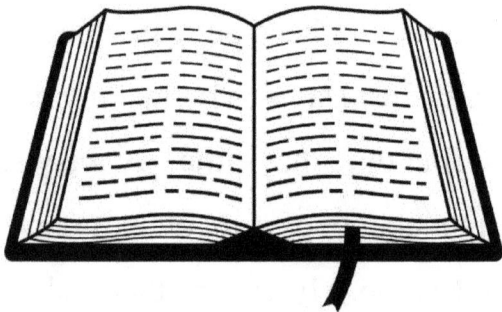

# Chapter Five

I attended Holmes Elementary school, across the busy street on 12<sup>th</sup> Avenue, with my sister, Bonnie, who was two years younger. My first-grade teacher's name was Ms. I.K. Johnson. She had a hump on her back, and she would slap you on your back if you misbehaved. I took piano lessons from Ms. Higgs, who would hit your fingers with a wooden stick if you played the wrong key. My sister, Bonnie, didn't finish her lessons with Ms. Higgs because she didn't like that. It didn't happen to me too many times. I learned my notes and was getting hit less and less.

I attended Allapattah Elementary and Allapattah Junior High after we moved to a house on 47 Terrace. It was just the four of us, my dad, mom, sister, and me. At the age of twelve, my parents divorced, and my dad moved out.

My sister Bonnie and I would pretend we were grown-ups with long hair. We changed our names to Regina and Betty. When we had to wash dishes, we would pretend we were on a commercial and advertise the liquid detergent. That made the time go faster while we took turns washing dishes. We would put towels on the backs of our heads and have them lie down on the back as if they were long, straight hair. We would swing them back and forward. It was just the two of us for a long time and we would make up different things to do to make doing our chores easier. As we got older, we would share in the chores, washing dishes every other day or vacuuming. Saturdays were our clean up days. Mom would get us up early, and right after having our breakfast, we would start doing our chores. It was a deep cleaning on Saturday, mopping the floors and cleaning out closets. We would always clean the floor on our knees. Today, I still clean my floors on my knees. This is something mom would always make us do on those Saturday clean-up days. She instilled into me that cleanliness is next to Godliness. I learned how to clean and cook at an early age. I would watch my dad come home and cook. He taught me how to cook different dishes. I would watch him, and he would let me help with the meals. On Saturdays, Dad would get peas and Bonnie and I would have to shell the peas, pick the greens, and shuck the corn on the cob. We had no choice. Not that we liked doing it, but we sure liked eating it at Sunday dinner. Collard greens were my favorite, along with fried corn, and field peas. It was a treat to have my favorites on Sunday.

My dad had a guitar, which he played on the weekends. He would have Bonnie and me sing and do little steps while he played the guitar. Mom would be in the bedroom talking on the phone to her friends. We would practice every weekend and some nights. Bonnie sang soprano and I sang alto. Dad would lead songs and we were the background. We would attend church events that had several singers on program. We performed at different churches, and we enjoyed it. Practice was the main thing we did on the weekends. Dad would come up with the songs and we would rehearse them, practicing our steps together. My dad loved listening to different quartet-style singers. He would buy all their records and albums, The Mighty Clouds of Joy, The Soul Stirrers. He would play their music all the time at the house. We would go and visit some of their performances at different churches. I grew to love that type of singing too.

I remember our dad making us eat bread for every meal. I told him when I turned twenty-one that I wasn't eating any more bread. I do not like bread as a result from him making us eat it all the time. I remember going to a family reunion and he said something to me like, Jeanette, I do not see any bread on your plate. I told him then I wasn't going to eat bread anymore because he made us eat it when we were younger. He was so surprised about that and said he did not know he caused me not to eat bread anymore. Everyone who knows me, knows that I do not eat bread. That is so funny, how when you become an adult, you are burned out on certain foods and habits that you had as a child.

Family reunions were big in our family. We would travel to Georgia almost every year, where my aunts would make sure we had a family reunion. We had family all over, from Connecticut, Georgia, and Florida. The food was cooked by my aunts who cooked very well. Sometimes we would have chitterlings. On Thanksgiving Day, we would go to our Aunt Louise's house in Florida and have a Thanksgiving feast. Most families that lived in Florida and some from Georgia would come. I was always the last person at the table. I eat slowly and would sit there and take my time and eat, to be left at the table every year, the last one sitting there. When I finished, I would help clear the table or sometimes they would clear the table around me, but I would help wash dishes. The food was always good.

# Chapter Six

Birthday parties were one of the main events we both looked forward to. Bonnie's birthday was in October, mine in September. We would have birthday parties together, maybe right after September 7. We would invite our cousins and friends in the neighborhood. Every year, as far back as I can remember, we would have a party. It was always with one big cake, with both of our names on it. One year, we each had our own birthday cake.

I remember Mom and Dad hugging and kissing. When they did that, Bonnie and I would surround them with our arms and hug them while they hugged and kissed.

In the summertime, we would always go to Georgia and visit my dad's family. I had a lot of uncles and aunts and cousins. They lived in the country. Sometimes we would take our grandparents with us. We loved going to the country. Our family treated us nice. They would cook for us, and my aunts would take care of us, cook, wash our clothes, and buy us things from the country store. Our cousins would play with us, and we would always take gifts for them. I remember one year, leaving my doll at one of my cousin's houses. When we returned home, we realized we had left it and told her to keep it for herself. Our uncles worked in the field. They lived on a plantation and did not go to school. They could play with us in the evening, after they did their chores. They would pick cotton and work in the field, planting vegetables.

There was always something cooking at my Aunt Minnie Pearl's house; she was the oldest girl in my dad's family. My Aunt Louise and Aunt Cora Bell would cook, too.

My uncles' names were Willie Joe Washington and Glenn C. Washington. My aunts' names were Minnie Pearl Williams, Louise

Mansfield, Cora Bell Singleton, and Ethel Williams.

Sometimes, our uncles and aunts would visit us. I remember my Uncle Junior visiting us and bringing his wife with him. They stayed with us for a little bit, then moved into their own house.

I remember my aunt who lived in New York came and visited us. She brought her baby, my cousin, with her. She stayed a little while too. They called her Baby Sister. My mom and Aunt Cora Bell were good friends and would talk all the time.

# Chapter Seven

After so many arguments, my mom and dad got a divorce. I was twelve years old.

After the divorce, Dad would come and pick us up every weekend, and if not, then every other weekend. We would go bowling and go to the movies. Most of the time, we went to church on Sunday. When Dad first moved out, he lived in the front of the house of a church member of ours, a good friend to him. He rented the front part of the house to him. Then Dad moved into his own apartment.

He bought his first house but rented it when he bought his second house. The second house was in Norwood; he had two big Doberman dogs and a basement. He bought a third house that had red carpet and an outside pool. Dad decided to sell that house and moved to Pelham, Georgia, in the country. He plants vegetables and has a few pecan trees. He shares them with his friends.

We have another sister. Her name is Keisha Gray. She lives in Miami with her mom. Keisha was born on November 11. We met Keisha as a toddler. As she got older, she would come over on the weekends when we visited our dad. We would do things together. Keisha was very shy and quiet. Keisha now has two children, a boy and a girl.

My boyfriend, James, asked me to marry him. I went to my dad to tell him and ask him to give me away. He did not, because he said he didn't know I had a boyfriend in the first place. I didn't share those things with him. My dad was very strict and didn't want us talking to boys when we were younger. When I met my boyfriend, I didn't introduce him to my dad, nor did I tell Dad I had a boyfriend.    My grandfather, Joseph Pierce, gave me away at my wedding.

My mom got a job as a beautician. She was a very smart lady. She could learn how to do things quickly. She always kept up with her license from Sunlight Beauty School, where she and a few other ladies graduated. She worked in a white salon in Dadeland, south of Miami. She would take me there to take rollers out of the clients' hair and sweep the floor from the hair that fell on the floor after a hair trim. Mom was the shampoo girl during that time. I remember getting tips, which I saved and spent some of the money at the mall. That was my first small job, working with my mom at the hair salon. Then Mom went to school, Barry College, to be a teacher. She got a job with Miami Dade County Schools as an educator. She first worked at an elementary school, then transferred to a high school, Miami Jackson High, then an alternative school, MacArthur North. Mom worked with Mr. Moncur, and Ms. Washington worked at that school, too. She befriended many other workers there, too.

Mom fostered several groups of children until they were grown. There were four children from my mom. It was myself, Jeanette Louise, Bonnie Denise, Marilyn Patrice and John Collis Jordan, Jr. (John was a junior, his father was John Collis Jordan, Sr.) John worked as a Correctional Officer at Miami Dade Corrections, where he met his wife, Diane. Marilyn went to Dover, Pennsylvania, to New Life for Girls. After graduation, she stayed as a counselor for several years. She decided to move to Atlanta, with me and my boys. I was going through a divorce from their father, James Sherrell Wallace, who lived with his sister and her husband, when we met. The Amicas had three children, one boy, Angelo, and two girls, Marquetta and Felecia. My sister-in-law and brother-in-law, Charles and Naomi Amica, were very nice to me. The boys and I would go over there almost every Sunday after church. She would cook and make the most delicious cakes. I met them when we would visit my cousins on 66 street in Miami, the Mitchells. There were nine sisters. We would visit them in the summertime and sometimes stayed all day.

# Chapter Eight

I was in high school, working at Sunny Furniture Company as a receptionist and a credit investigator, when I met James. Checking people's credit before they purchased furniture, that was my first real job. I worked there after school and on Saturdays. After I graduated from school, I would work there some summers. I got this job through a work study program in high school. I attended Miami Jackson High School, where I was in the chorus for four years. Mr. Roscoe Speed was the music teacher. He was a very talented individual who took us to the concerts where we performed in the Opera cast of "Aida." We sang and posed as the slaves in the musical. It was so interesting and fun. We performed six times. We always attended competitions among the other high schools. I also entered in the Miami Jackson pageant. I did not win, but my sister Bonnie and her friend Corine were my backups for my talent presentation. We sang an old song. I was lead singer and they were my backups. I graduated in 1972. I hung with the girls that were larger than I. You see, I was a skinny little girl and realized if I hung with the big girls, no one would bother me. I was right. I never was in a fight, and no one ever bothered me. I remember running home from school whenever there was a fight that was going to break out. They weren't fighting me; I just didn't like to see fights or for anyone to get hurt.

I would go to Miami on spring breaks all the time, along with other holidays. The youth fair would be in town, and we would attend there, too. Mom and I would visit family and friends. I would bring James, Jamaal, and Tasha with me. As the boys got older, I would bring Tasha only. Mom had many friends over the years. We would always make a day to visit family and friends. We made sure we get some conch to eat and other foods that we liked.

Mom had a doctor, eye, and foot doctor appointments. At the foot doctor, they soaked her feet in a big tub of warm water. She said it felt so good. I would make sure I made the appointments so I could go to Miami and take her.

I would always leave the following day. This one day, I picked up Bonnie because I had bought her some food from Snappers. She also wanted to go to a thrift shop to purchase a microwave. While we were there, a lady told her she had purchased an iron from Walmart and didn't like it. She would give it to her if she took her home, which was just around the corner. We took the lady to her place, and she went in to get the iron and brought it back to us at the car. We stopped at Ms. Smith's to drop off some food that I purchased from Winn Dixie. I would always get Ms. Smith a dinner and drop it off to her house before I went back home. Ms. Smith was a longtime friend of mine, who worked with me at an elementary school, years ago. Ms. Smith is still a dear friend, who turned one hundred years old in 2022. I dropped Bonnie back home. Her daughter, Sheba and Sheba's son, Mikel, came by to visit with Mom, then they dropped me off to the airport.

After Mom's service, I got a little teary-eyed. I'm going to miss coming down to Miami and hanging out with my mom. We would go to Red Lobster for her birthday and sometimes get fried conch—she liked the lemon pepper on it. After doctor appointments, we would stop at Burger King and purchase a Whopper, fries, and a drink.

On the last week, I came down because my brother called and said Mom didn't look too good, and he didn't like how she was breathing. It was confirmed by the hospice nurse who was there at the house, whom we had gotten maybe a week before, while Ms. Lisa, her caregiver, was off on summer break. The nurse said that Mom's oxygen level was low. My brother called the ambulance, they took her to the hospital, and she was admitted in ICU. The ICU doctor called and talked to me about "no CPR or DNR" not being signed. She didn't feel comfortable putting Mom through an uncomfortable and aggressive state. She informed me that Mom was an eighty-six year old woman and that putting her body through that much pain to revive her when it might be the same result was not a good idea. Mom was transferred to the hospice wing, and I asked for an IV to be put in so she could have fluids. The doctors explained that it could cause other problems, such as swelling, but they did it anyway for a day or two. Coming down to Miami, we were able to visit Mom four hours per day, and I would take my sister-in-law to work then use her car to visit Mom every morning. I would stay over my four hours sometimes, but they didn't say anything to me. I would wash her face, put lotion on her body and talk to her about what was going on with me. I told her the story that she always told me every year, about how her and my dad would go to the beach on Labor Day, and on this particular Labor Day, she was pregnant with me, her firstborn. When they came home from the beach, she lay across the bed and rested, but when she woke up, her water had broken. They took her to the hospital—at that time, Range Funeral Home had an ambulance service that took people to the hospital. I was born the next morning around five, on September 7, 1954. That date was coming up again, 2021, Monday, Labor Day. Before I went to the hospital, I thought I would pick up some party favors and decorate Mom's room for my birthday party the following day on Monday, Labor Day. I reinvented that day, sixty-seven years ago, by going to the beach before going to the hospital. I purchased a Subway sandwich, one of the items I used to buy for Mom when I would visit. I also purchased some coconut water, and I brought a blanket and a towel and sat on the sand. I ate my sandwich and drunk my coconut water, trying to imagine how my mom and dad enjoyed that day at the beach. I left the beach and went to the hospital. I purchased the items and decorated the room. I had a picture of Mom on the table and made a poster that said, "Happy Blessed Day, Jeanette." I put the poster on the wall. I had hats, blowing whistles and candy.

My husband, Mr. Norris, surprised me and came in the next morning to Miami, to spend my birthday with me.

I didn't know it, but he had taken the rest of the week off. After I picked him up from the airport, we stopped at two bakeries to get two slices of cake. When we got to the hospital, Mr. Norris prayed for Mom. He recited the 23rd Psalms, I sang "Jesus Loves Me" and we sang "Happy Birthday" to me.

I kissed Mom and told her I loved her. I also said, "Close your eyes and rest. Mom, go to sleep, get some rest." I kissed her all over her face, and said I love you again. We left and went to the beach. There was a young man on the beach who oversaw umbrellas, lounges, and canopies. He blessed us with a canopy because we didn't have enough cash. A week later, we went back to the beach and saw the same guy and we were able to give him a ten dollar tip. He didn't know what we'd been through. The next morning, the phone rang about 4:55. It was the hospital, telling me that Mom had passed ten minutes before and that we could come to the hospital to see her and sign some papers. I told my brother, who was on his way to work. We all got in the car, went to pick up Bonnie, and went to the hospital to see Mom. My brother and sister-in-law went first, then Bonnie and I went. My sister, Bonnie, said goodbye to Mom and kissed her. She got a little emotional. I just looked at her because

I had said my goodbyes the day before. God saw fit to allow me to have my mom at my birthday party in her room. I am so grateful and blessed. She was resting. We made preparations for her service. We had to meet with the funeral home and the cemetery. I had to pick out Mom's outfit that she was going to wear. Mr. Norris drove around, and I went looking and purchased the outfit. Mom's service was wonderful. She looked peaceful. All her family and friends attended. Some people spoke highly about Mom. All the grandchildren and great-grandchildren were there. We had buttons made and the program was nice. There was a poem in it from the grandchildren. When we arrived at the cemetery, the funeral director said his remarks and thanked everyone for coming on behalf of the family. My dad sang a hymn which was very nice, and we said our goodbyes.

We went back to the house, where family and friends came over to eat and sit outside in the yard to fellowship. I fried some conch fritters from the batter that Mr. Walter provided for us. They were eating them as fast as I was frying them.

We, as a family, feel we did all we could to take care of our mom, and I am grateful that we were able to do it.

We gave her, her flowers while she was here on earth.

I thank God for my best birthday party EVER!! Even though I had a birthday party every year during my childhood, my sixty-seventh birthday was the best birthday I have had because it was with my MOM, the day before she went to be with the LORD. I will never forget that special moment.

REST IN PEACE, MOM!!

# **<u>AFFIRMATIONS</u>**

Mom would always say, "Mama may have, Papa may have, but God bless the child that has his own."

# **<u>SCRIPTURES</u>**

My mom's favorite scripture was:

The Lord is my shepherd; I shall not want.  Psalms 23:1


He that dwelleth in the secret place of the most High shall abide under the shadow of the Almighty.  Psalms 91:1

# QUESTIONS

What memories do you have of your family that you will never forget?

What are some of the favorite foods your family used to cook that you still enjoy?

Did your family get together for family reunions?

Who in your family was the life of the party?

# **Notes**

_____

_____

_____

_____

_____

_____

_____

_____

_____

_____

_____

_____

_____

_____

_____

_____

_____

# REFLECTIONS

I remember my grandmother, every Sunday, would bake cakes, pies, or peanut brittle.

I remember my grandfather cooking Sunday dinners.

The smell was all over the house.

I remember my dad, barbecuing ribs in the backyard on some Saturdays. He would always put hot dogs on the grill for the kids.

I remember my mom, putting candy curls in our hair for Easter Sunday. She would decorate eggs and my dad would hide them. We would search for the golden egg.

At the breakfast, lunch, or dinner table, before we ate, my dad would have us take turns and recite a Bible verse.

During Christmas time, my mom and dad would decorate the tree with lights and ornaments and the outside of the house with lights and spiritual nativity decorations.

# **REFLECTIONS FROM THE**

# **GRANDCHILDREN**

One of the fondest memories I have of my grandmother was when I experienced snow for the first time. I was only six years old, and my mother and grandmother were with me. We were in Washington, D.C., waiting for a layover flight, when it started snowing. As a Miami native, I had never seen snow before and I was beyond excited. My grandmother shared in my excitement, and we spent the day enjoying the winter wonderland together. Her joy was contagious, and she made the experience even more special for me. I will always cherish that memory and the bond that we shared that day.

James Wallace Jr.

I remember going to family reunions with Grandad. No matter where my mom and I lived, Grandad would come and pick me up and take me with him and Ms. Betty. I enjoyed getting away and seeing family in another state. The best part was when Grandad came around with his camera. I would try to think, *what I am going to say,* before he came to me. "Hello, young lady, what is your name? Where are you visiting from?" I would get nervous every time. Now I see myself doing the same thing when at family gatherings.

Sheba Deniece Stubbs

At eighty-eight years old, my grandad is a true inspiration. Despite his advanced age, he still possesses a level of energy and vitality that many people half his age would envy. He takes care of his farmland and works tirelessly to maintain it, something that requires a great deal of physical stamina and endurance. Even long drives, lasting hours at a time, don't faze him; he approaches them with the same gusto and enthusiasm that he brings to everything else in life.

What's truly remarkable about my grandad, though, isn't just his physical abilities. It's his attitude and outlook on life. He's one of the most positive, cheerful people I know, and I've never once seen him upset or angry.

Even in the face of adversity, he maintains an unwavering optimism and determination that's truly inspiring.

As a member of my family, my grandad is a positive role model for all of us. He embodies the values of hard work, dedication, and perseverance, and serves as an example of what it means to lead a fulfilling and meaningful life. Seeing him in action, has taught me the importance of staying active and engaged, even as we get older, and has motivated me to strive for the same level of success and accomplishment that he has achieved.

Overall, my grandad is an incredible human being, and I feel truly blessed to have him in my life. His positivity, energy and resilience serve as a constant source of inspiration and motivation, and I can only hope to emulate his example as I grow older.

James Wallace, Jr.

When I was fourteen years old, I visited my granddad down in Georgia on his farm. He took me around on his go kart and showed me how to drive it around the farm. Afterwards, I really wanted to learn how to play pool since my friends all knew how to play except for me. I asked my grandad if he could teach me, and of course, he said yes. We spent hours in the garage, practicing. I love that my grandad is always up for anything and is always gracious with his time.

Latasha Norris Solaris

My grandmother's house is the house
where we always stayed and visited
when we went to Miami. We would
always go to Grandma's school where
she worked and visited her until school
was out. We would get hot sausage
from the neighborhood store and stop
the ice cream truck for ice cream. He
would ring his bell coming down the

street and we would run out, and my grandma would pay for everyone's ice cream. My grandmother loved when we came and visited. She would make sure we had a good time.

Jamaal Wallace

"One thing I can remember about Grandma is her generosity. When she would pick me up after school, I could always look forward to stopping to the store for a sweet treat on the way home."

John Jordan, Jr.

"I can remember that Grandma was very meticulous about her appearance. She was always dressed to impress!"

Nya Desir

# Pictorial

# Gallery

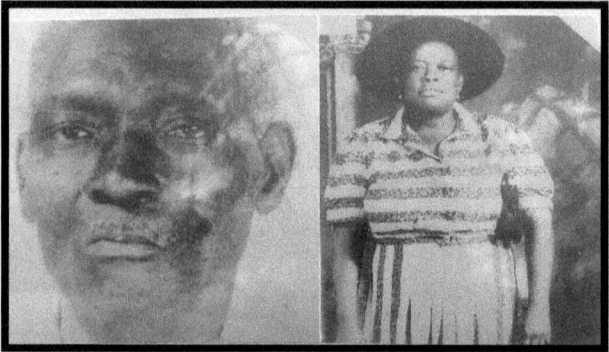

**Joseph and Carrie Levarity –**

**Great Grandparents**

**Emmit Davis - Grandfather**

**Isabell and Joseph Pierce -**

**Grandparents**

**Mom and Dad**

**Mom and Dad**

**Jeanette and Bonnie**

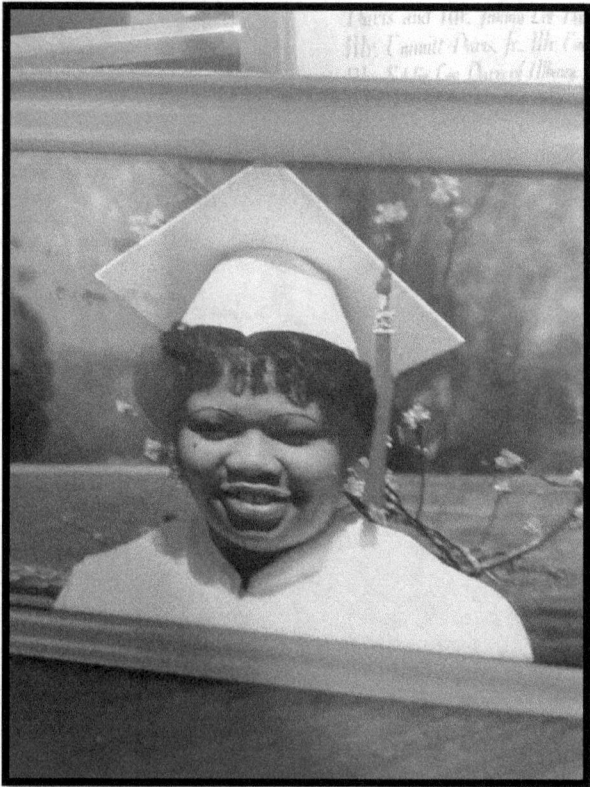

**Marilyn**

**Keisha**

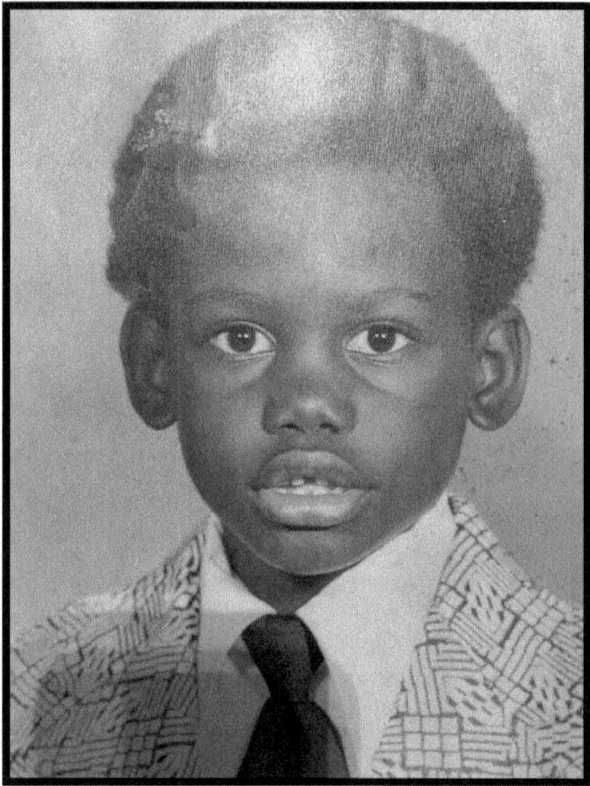

**John Collis Jordan, Jr.**

**Mom and Danielle**

**Dad Tasha and Mom**

**James, Jr. and Sheba**

**Mom, Ayanna, John, Jr., Mikel, Navah and Jasmine**

**Jamaal**

**Jeanette, Derrick, Dashawna,
Tasha and Monica**

# About the Author

Jeanette Davis Norris was born in Miami, Florida in 1954. She moved to Louisville, Kentucky in 2006. She was inspired to write this book about her parents before her mother passed in 2021. She reinvented the actions that occurred that day by going to the beach on Labor Day. Which was the same exact month and day, September 6, sixty-seven years ago. Her mom was nine months pregnant with Jeanette. They went to the beach that day and had a wonderful time.

When they returned, her mom lay across the bed to take a nap, to be taken by her water breaking, and was rushed to the hospital. Jeanette was born the following morning. September 6, 2021, on a Monday, Labor Day, Jeanette went to the beach. The next day, on her birthday, she came to the hospital to celebrate her birthday with her mom, not knowing this was going to be her last day with her. She decorated the hospital room with balloons, posters, and party favors. Jeanette remembers that day being an awesome day. She and her husband, Derrick, sang "Happy Birthday" and prayed. They had cake and her mom was there with her, opening her eyes, as if to let Jeanette know she was celebrating with her. This was a day